Create your own learning plan

Example: My learning plan for improving form filling.

I need to go through the following areas to make sure that I am getting them right:

1. Understanding different types of forms (Section 1)

2. Checking my completed forms (Section 4)

I need to increase my confidence and spend the most time on this area:

3. Completing forms effectively (Section 3)

Write your own learning plan here. The questionnaire on page 4 will help you get started.

_____

_____

_____

_____

_____

_____

_____

_____

_____

_____

_____

_____

_____

_____

_____

_____

_____

_____

_____

_____

Section 1

DIFFERENT TYPES OF FORMS

There are many different types of forms that we may be required to complete, either in the workplace or in day-to-day life. Some of these forms are simple and some are more complex.

Simple forms

These are forms that require only basic information, e.g. name, address and telephone number. They are usually easy to understand, well laid out and the instructions clear and simple.

Examples of simple forms are: an application for a library ticket, a company message form, a self-certification form for days off work.

Complex forms

If you are applying for a job or writing a report of an accident you are likely to have to complete a more complex form. These are forms that require more detailed information and lengthier answers.

Examples of more complex forms are: an accident report form, an application for training at your place of work, a passport application, an application for child benefit, a form for sending a fax message.

If you are having difficulty completing a form, it may be the form that is at fault and not you! Forms are sometimes badly designed and their instructions not always clear. Whatever the case, this booklet will help you to understand forms more easily.

Activity 1

Think about the forms you have had to fill in. What features make them difficult to complete and what features make them easy?

Tick the points that make form filling difficult for you and add any others in the space below:

- [ ] Understanding the words
- [ ] Following the layout
- [ ] Filling in the boxes
- [ ] Fitting my handwriting into the spaces provided
- [ ] Numbering of items
- [ ] The amount of information required
- [ ] Having to collect a lot of information

_____

_____

_____

Tick the points that make form filling easy for you and add any others in the space below:

☐ Words which are easy to understand
☐ Knowing where to write on the form
☐ Only personal details, e.g. name and address, being required
☐ Having enough space to write in
☐ Not having to find out a lot of information

_____

_____

_____

Activity 2

The form below requires personal details, which you are likely to be asked to provide on almost all forms. Note that sometimes you will be asked to fill in forms using only capital letters, while for others you may need to use ordinary handwriting. Always follow the instructions carefully. Complete the form, then look at the example given in the feedback section.

PERSONAL DETAILS
Please write clearly in BLACK INK and CAPITAL LETTERS.
SURNAME _____
FIRST NAME(S) _____
ADDRESS _____
_____
_____
_____
DATE OF BIRTH _____
SIGNED _____ DATE _____

You will find the feedback to this activity on page 20.

Key Learning Points

- Many forms are simple and require only basic information such as your name and address.

- Complex forms, such as applications for a passport or for employment, require more detailed information.

- If you have difficulty in completing a form this may be caused by the form being badly designed or unclear rather than your lack of skill.

- There are other difficulties that people may experience when completing forms. These include: not having enough space to write in, not understanding the numbering system, and not having the required information at hand.

IMPROVING FORM FILLING. LEARNING FOR WORK Series. © Workbase Training

Section 2

UNDERSTANDING THE WORDS USED ON FORMS

Filling in forms becomes much easier if you understand the meaning of the words used. The next activity will help you to become familiar with some of the words frequently used on forms.

Activity 3

Below are some words which often appear on forms. Write in the meaning against each word. Use a dictionary if you are unsure of the meaning of any of the words.

Word(s)	Meaning	Word(s)	Meaning
Referee		Previous	
Place of residence		Location	
Remuneration		Forename	
Maiden name		Occupation	
Marital status		Qualifications	
Employment		Next of kin	
		Surname	

You will find the feedback to this activity on page 20.

Completing a job application form

In Activity 4 you are asked to complete a job application form. This is one of the most important forms that people are required to complete. Here are a few tips which you may find useful before you complete the form.

- Always read and follow any instructions given to you on or with the form.
- Complete the form in block letters and black ink or in type unless you are asked to do otherwise.
- If you are asked to demonstrate that you have a particular skill, explain how you have previously used this skill. Use job-related examples if you can, but if this is not possible then use examples from non-work activities, e.g. helping at a playgroup.
- Try to write neatly and legibly.
- Complete the form in light pencil first of all, then rub it out and write over it in ink.
- Use a dictionary if you are unsure of the meaning of any of the words on the form.

Activity4

A job you are interested in has been advertised in your local paper. You have decided to apply. Choose an appropriate job title and complete the following application form in BLOCK CAPITALS and black ink, using your own background. (The purpose of this activity is to give you practice in completing a job application.)

Application for the post of _____

at _____

Surname _____

(Mr/Mrs/Miss/Ms) Delete where not applicable

Forenames _____

Maiden name (where applicable) _____

Date of birth _____

Address _____

_____

_____ Postcode _____ Telephone no. _____

Form continued opposite ...

IMPROVING FORM FILLING. LEARNING FOR WORK Series. © Workbase Training

Details of any special training/apprenticeship, development, etc. with dates and qualifications held

_____

_____

_____

_____

Are you registered under the Disabled Persons Act?   YES/NO

If yes, please give registration number _____

Current and Previous Employment
Please give details of your current and previous employment. If you are not in paid employment, please give details of any voluntary or other activities you are involved in. Start with your current or most recent activity or employment. Use extra sheets if necessary.

Position and brief description of duties	Employer's name, address and telephone number, and name of person to contact	Date commenced employment (From)	Date finished employment (To)

*You will find an example
form on page 20.*

Key Learning Points

☐ It is important that you understand what information is required on a form.

☐ Certain words are used frequently on forms. Such words include: surname, marital status, next of kin, occupation. It is important that you understand the meaning of these words.

☐ You need to be familiar with the words and phrases that commonly appear on job application forms.

☐ Sometimes the information you are asked for will be specific. For example, a form used to request work clothes would require details of sizes. An application form to join an organisation's pension scheme would require details of age, partner and salary. There is no need to worry about this specific information because there will generally be someone to give advice.

Section 3 COMPLETING FORMS EFFECTIVELY

Whatever types of forms you are required to complete, there are some general rules that will help you tackle this task and enable you to do it in the most effective way. Read the tips below.

Tips for filling in forms

- Allow enough time, so that you can make a good job of filling in the form.
- Read through the form and look up any unfamiliar words in your dictionary.
- Collect together any documents and information you need.
- Do a rough draft first.
- Ask someone to check what you have written if you are not sure whether it is the right information.
- Write in pencil first, then go over it in pen and rub out the pencil marks when you're sure it's right.
- Write N/A (not applicable) beside any questions which do not apply to you.
- When you have finished, use the form-filling checklist on page 18 to check that you haven't forgotten anything.
- Make a copy of your completed form so that you have a reminder of what you have written. This will also help you next time you have to fill in a similar form.

Activity 5

You would like to apply for a training course in computing. Using the tips above, complete the form below, then look at the example on page 22.

APPLICATION FOR COMPUTER TRAINING

Name: _____

Job title: _____ Section: _____

Extension number: _____

Home address: _____

_____ Postcode: _____

Form continued on page 14 ...

Telephone number: _____ Date of birth: _____

State briefly the training you would like to do and why.

_____

_____

_____

Describe briefly any training you have received.

_____

_____

_____

How would you like to study (e.g. in a group, self-study, one to one)?

_____

_____

_____

Is there any other information you would like to add?

_____

_____

_____

Key Learning Points

- ☐ Take your time when completing a form to ensure that you make a good job of it.

- ☐ Read through the whole form and any instructions that go with it before attempting to fill it in.

- ☐ Collect all the necessary information and do a rough draft first.

- ☐ Write in pencil on the form first of all and ask someone to check it for you.

Section4 CHECKING YOUR COMPLETED FORMS

The more practice you have at filling in and checking forms, the better you will become at it.

Once you have completed a form, it is vital to check that you have:

- filled in all the relevant sections of the form
- not made any spelling or punctuation errors
- put down the correct information
- signed the form if necessary.

On page 18 is a checklist to help you ensure that you have completed your forms effectively.

Self-certification forms

If you are absent from work because of illness you will usually have to complete a self-certification form when you return to work. This will also apply if you are absent for any other reason. Such forms are normally straightforward but it is important to fill them in correctly.

Activity6

Complete the self-certification form on the next page on behalf of John Brown, using the following details:

John Brown works for A1 Computers; he is based at the Watford site. He has been off work for three days because he strained his back while he was moving computer equipment to a client's premises. He informed his manager, Dilip Sangit, when he returned from the client's premises on Monday, 17 May and Dilip sent him immediately to the doctor. The doctor recommended that he rest in bed for three days to prevent his back pain from getting worse. John informed his manager by telephone, after visiting the doctor, that he would be away for three days from the following day. He started his sick leave on Tuesday, 18 May and his last day off work was Thursday, 20 May.

You will find the feedback to this activity on page 22.

SELF-CERTIFICATION FORM

Please complete on your first day back at work:
If you were absent because you were sick complete Section 1.
If you were absent for any other reason (for example, family illness, domestic problems) complete Section 2.

Employee name _____
                        (First name)   (Surname)

Place of work _____

1. Sickness

My illness started on _____ the _____ of _____ 19_____
                        (Day)   (Date)   (Month)

and ended on   _____ the _____ of _____ 19_____
                        (Day)   (Date)   (Month)

I was therefore away through illness for a total of _____ days.

I suffered from:

_____

_____

_____

_____

I have consulted a doctor: Yes/No
A medical certificate is required for sickness lasting longer than 7 days.

2. Absence for other reasons

I was absent from work from _____ the _____ of _____ 19_____
                                 (Day)   (Date)   (Month)

                      to _____ the _____ of _____ 19_____
                                 (Day)   (Date)   (Month)

I was therefore absent for a total of _____ days.
My absence was due to:

_____

_____

_____

_____

Accident report forms

If you were the only person there when an accident happened at work, you would probably be asked to complete an accident report form. Do not worry if this seems difficult, there will always be someone to help.

Activity 7

Fill in the accident report form below, using the following details:

Owain Jones, aged 32, works for A1 Computers. He and his colleague, John Brown, aged 50, were delivering computer equipment to a client at an industrial estate in Slough on Monday, 17 May. While John was unloading the computer equipment from the van, he strained his back. Owain had to help him and then had to carry the remaining equipment into the client's premises by himself. The delivery took place at 9.30 in the morning and, after the delivery was completed, both Owain and John returned to their base at High Road, Watford. John reported the incident to their manager, Dilip Sangit. John was sent to the doctor to have his back examined. Owain Jones was asked to complete an accident report form.

ACCIDENT REPORT FORM

Please print

Date of accident _____ Time of accident _____

Name of person involved _____

Status or job title if an employee _____
(e.g. employee, visitor, contractor)

Name and address of employer _____

Describe how the accident occurred and what injuries were sustained.

_____

_____

_____

_____

_____

Form continued on page 18 ...

Name(s) of witness(es) to the accident _____

_____

Signed _____

Please print name _____

Senior staff on duty at the time of the accident

_____

Date _____

After this form has been completed it should be sent to the Personnel Department

CIB Claim Ref. _____

You will find the feedback to this activity on page 23.

Form filling checklist

Below is a list of points to help you check that you have completed your forms effectively. Use the list each time you fill in a form.

- Could someone else read it?
- Have I followed all the instructions?
- Have I answered every question?
- Is all the information correct?
- Have I put N/A if the question does not apply?
- Are my answers relevant?
- Have I made a copy of the completed form for reference?
- Have I checked it for errors?

If you can answer 'yes' to most of these questions then you are completing your forms correctly.

Key Learning Points

☐ Make sure that you read through your form after you have completed it.

☐ Ask someone to check your rough draft and then your completed form when you have finished.

☐ Try using the checklist in this section. If all your answers are 'yes' your form will be ready to send off or hand in.

Mini Project

Most of the form-filling techniques described in this booklet will apply to any type of form. If you want to improve your form-filling skills even further, collect some forms from work or from a post office and practise filling them in. You could use:

- job application forms
- self-certification forms
- training application forms
- passport forms
- TV licence forms
- holiday booking forms
- bank deposit/withdrawal forms

Action Plan

Take another look at the list of form-filling tips on page 13. Write down below those tips you want to remember for the future.

FeedBack toActivities

FEEDBACK TO ACTIVITY 2

PERSONAL DETAILS

Please write clearly in BLACK INK and CAPITAL LETTERS.

SURNAME ___DUTA___

FIRST NAME(S) ___RITA___

ADDRESS ___21 ACACIA AVENUE, BACKNALL,___

___HERTS.   SG1 2AJ___

DATE OF BIRTH ___21/05/72___

SIGNED ___*signature*___ DATE ___11/05/99___

FEEDBACK TO ACTIVITY 3

Word	Meaning
Referee	person who will provide information about applicant
Place of residence	Home address
Remuneration	salary or earnings
Maiden name	a woman's surname before marriage
Marital status	whether single, married, widowed, etc.
Employment	work
Previous	before or former
Location	place
Forename	first name or given name
Occupation	type of work
Qualifications	exams passed, certificates gained
Next of kin	nearest relative
Surname	family name

FEEDBACK TO ACTIVITY 4

Complete the following application form in BLOCK CAPITALS and black ink.

WESTFIELD BOROUGH COUNCIL
Application for the post of ___CLERICAL ASSISTANT___
at ___RAYNES PARK LIBRARY___

Form continued opposite ...

IMPROVING FORM FILLING. LEARNING FOR WORK Series. © Workbase Training